To H
with love

14.10.20

Y
POEMS OF SEPARATION

First published in 2020 by The Artel Press, Liverpool
www.theartelpress.co.uk

Copyright © Angie Pyman 2020

ISBN 978-0-9926035-6-4

The author's moral rights have been asserted in accordance with
the Copyright, Designs and Patents Act 1988

Printed by Imprint Digital, Devon

*To Mark, Chris and Holly
for making it happen.*

Acknowledgements

I am deeply grateful to my tutors at Warwick: Michael Hulse, Maureen Freely and Will Eaves, who were not only accomplished and engaging teachers, but who also supported me following the death of my father, and attendant family crises, during my Masters year.

Thank you to Lynne Rees and Patience Agbabi at the University of Kent, who were my first poetry tutors. In 2006, Patience and Michael Symmons Roberts taught at an Arvon Foundation course on The Poetic Sequence and opened my eyes to how the poems in a collection should strike notes off each other and bring wider perspectives to the reader.

Thanks also to John Elcock at The Artel Press, not only for having faith in the poems, but also for his guidance and tact.

And finally, a shout-out to Susan Elliot Wright, Sue Wilsher and Alison Burnside. Our workshopping sessions were a joy. Amazingly, several years on, we are all published authors.

CONTENTS

Y	1
Weightless	2
Lost In The Rainforest	4
Evacuation	6
Citronelle	7
Sécheresse	8
The Survivor	10
Walking The Way	11
Spirit Levels	12
The Scent Of Stones	13
Boy With Cockleshells	14
Safe Space	16
Fragile As Trust	17
Bone China	18
The Promise Of Green	19
A Ritual For Morning	23
Resting Place	24
The Year We Burned	25
Reliquary	26
Still Love	27
Evanescence	28
Sand Man	29

Hour Glass	31
Dervish	32
Sanctuary	34
Peking Knot	36
Mist At Dawn	37
Glimmering	38
Kindred Spirits	40
The Memory Of Angels	42
Runaway	43
Ties That Bind	44
Ebb Tide	45
Vigil	46
Eulogy For A Soldier	47
Lives We Have Lost	48
Mistral	50

Y

Turn it upside down
to make a cipher for a man,
no arms – the camera has grained
them out. He is
a wishbone, pulled
across a rift of trains.
You could sketch him
in the margin
of a history book:
a hieroglyph
serving the gods,
in some hoped-for afterlife.

Weightless

It begins with choices,
a reluctant leave-taking
of treasures.

The mundane selects itself –
pots, bedding – a return
to simplicity, as if

she's living backwards,
inhabiting an infant's dream.
If she had a screen

she could watch the sensation:
a slow-mo splintering of ice
away from cliffs. Exquisite.

The going's blind, the route
seems fenced with razor wire,
shaving her away, a millimetre

at a time. Blown across
the land until she makes
landfall; nothing but sand –

white against white, as if
it all might vanish and she would be left
upon the level desert.

Stirring the pot (how cherished now)
of alien rice, wielding a stick
stronger than the balsa

of her arm bone,
shrouded by the one last dress,
she knows it won't be long.

Lost In The Rainforest

Usually Daniel comes alone,
skimming the lagoon, coaxing the prow
of his heavy-hulled pirogue against the bank.

He leads us like pilgrims, on a path
overplaited with grass, tracking the way
through solemn guards of bamboo sheaves,

dipping under girders of angled palms. No-one
has told us what we'll find, and now we're here,
emerging from a screen of pygmy trees

into the nave; roofless, three walls dissolved
into forest debris. Tiers of crumbling pews
set out as in a clearing, wait two hundred years

for an open-air concert and its foreign star.
Purple brocade, gold frogging melt
upon his wooden throne

while crickets chant eternally.
So European, this place,

so strange and so familiar that I feel
we should have known them; the priest and bishop,
as if they were our kin, come here before us

to the Equator, its people and monsoons,
its pathways writ on water, its disease. I feel
I have become a stranger to myself.

Evacuation

For forty-eight hours,
one small suitcase
crouched by the door, carrying
— with the bare bones —
albums of six-by-fours

When it was over,
we compared what each
had spared space for,
and each had done alike:
packed the proof of his past,
the flesh on his skeleton.

Citronelle

I remember, after dinner, stepping out
into darkness warm with the sound of crickets,
to cull fistfuls of striped, narrow leaves.
Snipped into inch lengths,
  covered with boiling water,
they had the scent of lemon peel –
no hint of the pith or juice, and a taste

that rationed itself: so much needed
for even a teapot-full, the plant grudging,
self-contained, seemingly not African enough
to flourish in the soaking heat.
Though it was always dry when I cut the leaves,
and the paths empty, but for the dust.

Sécheressse

… whispers dryness. On sand,
snakes shift the ground, their hissing curves
a mockery of ripples. No spring
here, just dunes; even the dead leaves' rustle
a sere memory. Barren
earth and salt-whipped grasses
mark the land.

*

The drought's breath
spins a grid
of desiccated spaces.
At its centre, the sun.

Filaments cling, carry her
off her slight course
bestow her
on an alien coast.

Still her image
spirals away,
the future caught
in her cobwebbed face.

*

On these shores, the water
starts flesh-warm – no chill
to jolt your mind. Choose a beach that slopes
gentle as cotton, slipping into coolness
as into sleep. Skin is sense-free,
exchanging heat, trapping bubbles
on her arms' fine hairs
as if to gift her air.

She is ground glass
grained as saltwater
stranded as the tide recedes,

her skin, drought dried
paper, tracing
bones bleached light;

her skin, a reliquary
for her suppliant voice.

The Survivor

I saw him in Evelyn's treeless garden,
long limbs folded like birds' wings,

watching my daughter sift rivulets of sand
through dune-pale fingers. He didn't stay

in barracks with the guardiens, not even those
who came, like him, from the desert:

he was freelance. And silent, except with children.
It must have been strange to him, to live

on an island, where it seemed escape
was only to be had in flight, or by a careful stepping

across rafts of felled trees lifting on a slow tide.
Years have blurred him, as a sandstorm

abrades the skin. Perhaps he is there, still,
safe in the eye of it.

Walking The Way

On the way back, he took his knife
and dug it deep into the sandy soil
for a tuft of marram,
which he kept potted
by the backdoor, saying
they'd told their way by the grasses,
each land promising
the warmth of welcome by the push or yield
beneath their feet. He'd cover his eyes
and let the weft of landscape tell
the future through his leather soles.

Spirit Levels

Street level's the dividing line. Under the epidermis
her springs shrink in the heat; only the scent

of water oozes from her forty wounds.
She gazes up at coffee table legs,
  stalk thin and black,
laps up the lees from someone's shattered glass
and spits back dust, below the roar
of bikers on the Cours. We tamp her down,
stamp flat her layers of history, like tobacco.

Slide your finger nail beneath her skin,
prise up the brittle leaves
like Troy's striated cities, and you'll find
her Roman cisterns, her Jews' well.

In the banlieues
the alleys taste burnt, of cigars
waiting for the flicker of a match.

The Scent Of Stones

Ahmed ben Hammou
works the terracotta roofs
prising out split
half-cylinder tiles.

Almond to umber,
age-varied shades echo
the heaped apricots
of Rabat markets.

He sifts the mistral
with closed eyes, scenting
burnt-sweet odours:
cloves and cinnamon.

Around him, gardens
roost about the town:
sprung seeds, dropped
by migrating birds.

Boy With Cockleshells

His pack is russet leather. Worn to softness,
it lacks a decoration.
He has found three perfect shells,
whiter than the bones of saints, upon the beach
and shattered one already. There are strips of suede
waiting to marry another to the bag.

He's picked his way through father's workshop,
and mother's sewing box,
taken a coarse, old needle and a hammer.
The work is slow. Each careful tap
scratches a pinprick hole – he is afraid
to fracture ribs that once protected life.

Thirteen years old and he dreams of pilgrimage –
to dare the marsh and moonscape, see the thorns
from Jesus's crown, the amber box
that holds St Stephen's hand. More cruel by far
to print neat words at school then take the path
where countless others have: to Compostela
and further, to the rocks of Finisterre.

Chips fly off the shell and graze his hands.
Fragile as china, chalky with calcium,
one blow could crack the shell from end to end.

He finds a nail, strong in the stem, the point
sharp as a spike, and taps
softly through flesh, into the earth beneath.

Safe Space

Dawn starts up like a turbine, tipping
the new ones onto the lawn, copper perfect.

They are sharp-featured as winter, rolling out
along the pathways drawing a blueprint

of tracks in the snow, while we remain
at the window uncertain of them,

as if these were our own young,
limber and brazen, proofed against the light.

If we ventured out, they would lope
a tree's length away, then turn to stare.
Only their mother stays at the edge
of sight, close against the hedge,

leaving no mark where the leaves
have soaked the grass with water.

Fragile As Trust

Hold him on your palm, feel
sweat creep from your pores,
a stillness, tightening. Fear
seeps through.
His feet are hooks,
a soft dig into flesh.
Try to overcome
those bone memories.
He's used to rainforest, has no idea
what kind of landscape you are.
Hostile? Likely.
Better be ready for flight.

Bone China

Slick and unformed core of clay;
I place it on the wheel,
run fingers round its watered silk,
work the treadle, labouring
like a learning child.

Can it know the future, creature
of earth that turns beneath my hands?
Pliant yet resisting,
as if aware what contours best
would pleasure other eyes.

Last of all, a choice of glaze
and this is mine: blue as a poppy
from my heavy brushes
falling like mercury or honey
over kiln-fired curves.

Placed behind the glass, beyond
my unsure art. As a merchant might,
I wonder who will lift it
and whether it will chip or break
in another's keeping.

The Promise of Green

Heavy-eyed in the dark before dawn,
I hear the whisper of my mother's skirt
as she drops to her knees. Entreaty
has scoured her voice, to a sound like sand
scattering onto scree, or summer storms
gusting through wheat.

Muted shades emerge
above the valley: iron ore, pine grey
and sulphur. But the sky
is still hard-hearted blue.

She is praying for green, for me,
colour of a rich girl's dress, of grass
and trees that border water. It is said
in Paradise, the blessed
will wear clothes of rich, green silk.

Her life is like her prayers. She offers
promises, obedience, in trust
for food and future kindness,
in hope of trust returned.

*

I am the counterweight
In this exchange –
a rough green gem, traded
for the absence of a son.

She presses herb-stuffed pitta
into my slow hands. A man
she calls my *Uncle* lifts me
into a truck laden with others.

We travel in the dark,
are become nocturnal,
men as wolves and foxes.
Uncle calls me *Little Lamb*
strokes my head, offers
morsels of mutton.

We rest by day: bodies unfold
to clay or beaten earth,
in ruined house or barn.
We sleep or sit, sullen,
eat what's given, scavenge
but do not stray too far, hobbled
like donkeys by our need.

Seasons change around us,
roads flatten and echo
with engine noise, till we sniff salt
and freshness. Uncle discharges us
and his promise, discards us onto scrub.
I run, slide, scramble to the trucks,
bind myself beneath one. It is dark
as Hell above my head.

*

Metal and glare are waiting
on the other side: I see
no Paradise. Even the rain
is grey. They take me to a house
where warmth spills from the door
and strangers lead me
to a bed softer than fleeces.

That first night, water hammers on the roof,
muffling my father's cries. I dream
of absences: his and now mine
and wake to growing light.

Outside there's pasture, green
as any emerald.
I walk out and my feet sigh
into the wet grass: its chill,
its kindness; its colour
reflected in the rain which lies
scattered like tears across it.

For Z.A.

A Ritual For Morning

Sunrise, and the haze
lets pinpricks of light
pass sharp onto the mirror
as she begins: a mortar's measure
of powder and the pestle hefts,
working in the oil –

clove scented – for the temples'
cooling shadows. Now her fingers dip
slow into the tinder-box, bring out

a lily's worth of pollen, crushed
softer than his eyelid's threadbare satin,
brushing to bruise each cheek until

there is no telling dust
from skin. The lines of lip and bone
dissolve to leave the dulling mirror
empty – just the powdered trace
of ridges from her fingertips remain
upon the sill, scattering.

Resting Place

If you bury me, let it be here,
In the caves of pungent sand, where colours —
ochre, umber, rose —
swirl around each burial niche.
Lay me above the canyon, high enough
that the echo of the market traders is softer
than the beat of hawks' wings, and where footsteps
of the curious do not reach. Feel no regret
that your fingers have become too frail
to prise away the yellow bark:
Let the spice-shaded sandstone
surround my own, here where the dust
never settles, and the rock
whispers softly away from itself.

The Year We Burned

Summer stasis…
A vine's cracked web on the courtyard wall
Wind flickering the grasses.

The roof's flanks crumble, red frostbite,
a kind of gangrene –
they would let in the rain, but there is none.

Swifts in the plane trees, screaming
that it's time to leave.

We hide in our sand-coloured caves, watching
the hillsides burn.

They only seek the summer's light in cold countries,
clasp it do their Northern bones.

Its musicians the wind, plucking the cicadas' strings;
its colour, absence.

This is no time for pilgrimage.
Dust in air…

…and food. Dust and flux.
Silence outside. Inside, Babel.

Reliquary

Watching her sleep, he wondered –
if she should die tonight and yet
remain here till her flesh dissolved
and then be found upon some future wasteland,
could the nest of bones
construe her life – the metacarpals
fallen back, as if her grasp
were loosening upon some precious thing,
the vertebrae collapsing
as her skull tipped slowly off
the pillow; and the playful
skewing of one femur on the other?
Would they conjecture
from the bunched tarsals how her instep
cradled her heel?

And every shred
of evidence appraised, would they deduce
how recklessly she slept, how not a thought
had come to her of danger – how he shielded
her from harm, at least as much
as human flesh was able?

Still Love

No longer will he walk the fence edge, for his flesh
is melting off. Take a thick stalk
of charcoal and sketch in crumbling bones –
leave white space for the hollow of his flank;
fill out his tail, luxuriant by the ruin
of fragile vertebrae that arch like hands
steepled in prayer. His fur, sidelong,
is washed to rust by age or tongue.
Eyes water at his halting steps across
the table and the pained arrangement of his frame,
offering his bristled cheek for a caress –
he finds a hand's rough rubbing still sublime.

Evanescence

The old owners had fixed a strip against the wall,
behind the chrome taps and the worktop.
She held the knife and stood reflecting
before a still life of sliced tomatoes
or a colander of peas, as the river
breathed in and out of the house.

On misty days there were grey ghosts;
she never saw them come in, though the gulls
screamed a warning. She looked up from a book
and a cup of steaming chocolate, to see
clouds swirl together in the glass; didn't
pull the curtain or turn out the light.

For weeks the long track was empty.
She stayed in, went without, made do,
pretending she was marooned,
waiting for a passing yacht to rescue her.
But time and the tides were wrong.

Upstairs was different. She changed,
although the faded flowers did not.
In October, when the house was on fire
and the provisions finished,
she drifted away with the other flotsam,
still sitting with her back to the window.

Sand Man

He must have calved
from a dune one night
when equinoctial waves rose
and shifted the sand. I imagine him
heaving one shoulder free,
then the other, shucking off
the dune as if it were a wetsuit,
heading north, inland, as the wind
whipped away all trace
of his powdered steps.

Sundays, he goes back,
sails the sands at Pembury
when the tide's gone way out,
wheels cracking over the pebbles,
wind snapping at his heels.

He spits out questions
in his own unintelligible
dialect, like a lashing of rain,
but means no harm
as he straps on metal stilts,
reaches to the ceiling, rough-modelled,
tramping out his patch
working the plaster to flat calm.

There's a spring under his left heel
needs oiling – it squeaks
like a small creature lifted
by a raptor – but he hefts
hawk and float as in a dance,
clods of plaster dropping to the sheet,
like his own dun spawn.

Hour Glass

We hate solitude and gather together
all the time. Just think, when did you ever
see one of us alone? We crave the comfort
of rubbing all our surfaces on our own kind.

There's only one thing we love more:
water. We shrink ourselves into it,
cluster till we look like nuggets of iron ore,
then let it through, but slowly, slowly,

bathing in each drop, we cannot
delay it any longer. You, with your blood-softness
amuse us, each of you a plaything
full of folds and crevices, to probe and scratch.

You force us into alien shapes, pack us
into sacks to hold back tides and bullets,
but you'll not last long – your time here will be brief
As is the moment when a flake of snow

falls on the surface of a pool and is consumed.
Only one thing: when you sear us into glowing
globes and blow us into glass, then we are changed,
become like purest water, with a heart of ice.

Dervish

I was
fifteen, perhaps
when, tentative, I tried
a first revolution, one foot
risking

a step
from the launch pad
my long skirt beginning
to swirl faster, encompassing
a life

outside
objects were blurring
rainforests, skyscrapers
mingled. Within, I heard a faint
crying

yet I
did not slacken
spun steady as before
spirit extended pole to pole,
the ice

advanced
and then drew back
species were extinguished
and landscapes transformed to ruin
I spun

fearful
of the danger
in losing my balance
falling headlong away into
the storm

Sanctuary

Like a nun's cell,
small and square

On the far wall, a window
framed in unvarnished wood.
Beyond, a lawn, emerald
as spring after rain.
An herbaceous border
blurred by poppies.

Inside, neat and sparse:
flagstones hollowed by centuries,
a faded rug for bare feet
beside a single bed.
Cotton sheets, washed soft.

The bedstead was iron once,
but I wanted a headboard for reading,
so I changed it.

There are no books.

What else? An empty cupboard
and chest of drawers,
a carefully-ironed, white linen mat
with nothing placed on it; no possessions,
no knick-knacks from faraway places.

No dust.

This is my room.
And for now, it is ready.
I stand at the doorway, looking
but not entering. If I go in,
I will never leave.

Peking Knot

Feathers, heavy with silk, cascade
down full-skirted robes behind the glass.
An emperor's plumage,
finely wrought in Peking Knot,
glows in the sun,
where young fingers worked the needles
hour on hour; flesh pricked
and punctured, eyes aching,
for a few short seasons.
They called it *Blind Stitch*,
as the feathers
were blurred by salt
and the light
started to fade.

Mist At Dawn

I am the thief of touch, light-fingered,
crouching in the valleys,
coupling with the grass,
running my cheek against the fringe of bluebells,
merging with their ghosting scent.
I muffle the ewe's morning bleat
with memories of blurring Scottish hills
and velvet-statued stags. I soothe
the farmer's splintered gates. Hawks despise me
as I shelter small dawn creatures from
  their pinpoint eyes.
I am cold breath of water, brushing
dill-soft seaweed. I veil
high tide's unmoving gleam
and patterned fish beneath. Gulls linger
on the slipping varnish of a Devon yawl
to feel me shawl their feathers,
then lift, crying trickery, as I dissolve
below their wingtip,
beyond reach.

Glimmering

Here is where the light moves,
where the river's scimitar
carves its curves between

grasses, alders. Eddies,
thistled with catkins, carry
its brilliance downstream. And here

I dream the fish, pulsing
with thought, thrumming
in the current, taking his chance

against pike and rod.
I try to tease him out
with a feathered fly

as he holds, hovers, balances –
a needle seeking north.
And the line swirls,

looping against the clouds
like a child's firework
writing on the autumn sky,

till fish, river, rod,
shift, choreographed,
and he leaps up and out

fighting against my net
and thrashes there, wrestling
himself away from air.

Weighted. Graceless.

Kindred Spirits

My son has come looking for himself
in this village that hangs from the cliffs
as if it might fall into the sea.
The sands end here, under a wall
that bellies out to buffer the slow rolling waves
gliding in, patient, after their long haul
breasting the North Sea.

Across the narrow promenade is a building
of rough grey stone, and a single room
filled with twin behemoths of billiard tables
that crowd there, pine chairs against the walls.
There are monochrome photographs of the storm
of '53, when the road caved-in so far
another tide would have taken the foundations.

My son's sixth-generation ancestor
gazes from his portrait, over the reading room
he founded. We can fill in the rest of him,
for the men of this family are all alike:
tall, the same height to within an inch,
the same stretch of shoulder, only shades
of difference in the breadth of their chests.
Even their names – Walter, George, Frank –
tell of their Victorian solidity of shipping magnate,
research chemist, white-bearded city elder.

We stay in George's house, now a hotel,
and for his birthday, give my son a ring
engraved *fidelis fortis*, like the coat of arms
above the fireplace in the Pyman Bar.

It is a weekend of churchyards and stone angels,
of enduring ancestral homes reincarnated
for the new century. George would have approved

this pragmatism, even though his last ships
are those that sail across the stained-glass window;
and my son has come away with a story
of the boy who went to sea at ten years old.

The Memory Of Angels

I'd remembered little of the church itself –
only where it stood, high on Lythe Bank,
with the field lapping at its limits, more apt
for a watchtower than a place of worship.

But inside there was quiet and a warm, washed light.
We had the place to ourselves, were here
for family, your name in the register of graves:
East Quadrant, Conservation Area.

I went to look, remembering wings
and found them for you: their small fingers
cleaned white, as if scoured by the salt wind,
reassuring, just as required.

You knelt down beside *George aged 14*
and stroked aside the grass,
that lay in strands across the marble rim.

Runaway

Your breath makes ragged smoky patterns
against the hill, the hill you'll be running up
in ten minutes time. Where
will you be in the pack by then?
All the stretching, sprinting, slogging, sweating
now come to this.

Was there a time before the rigour,
the routine and dragging yourself
into trackie bums and spikes,
easing yourself out of the heated house
into the damp January park
where the grass plumps up with rain
and your feet slide over wormcasts?

Your shoulders hunch in jerky shrugs,
you bounce like a puppet, mouth twisted
down at the corners, skin white,
your teenage acne stands out
sharp like spattered mud,
stands out like you do
in the jostling line-up then the starter
lifts his pistol and you all stop. Crouch.
Clench hands into fists.
Spike elbows sideways.

And you're gone.

Ties That Bind

High summer in the creek. An ebbing tide
has pulled the clinging fingers of the sea
back till they break to lie in bars of light
along the rippled mud, while stilted birds
sketch ragged crisscross boundaries between
steel anchor chains whose links are wrapped in green.

We see the children come in twos and threes
down to the *voss*. Their jellied sandals slap
through pools, their yellow buckets pitch like tents
across the causeway. They take string,
knotted with leaded weights and bacon fat
then dip it in the stream, letting it hang
as long as they can bear, until at last
they pull and swing it up, seething with crabs.

The camera's in my hand as our boy takes
a careless step down from the causeway, shouts
to feel his toes splay in the oily grains
that ooze above his ankles. When he flails,
the mud clings on and drags him further down.

The photo shows them all caught in the act,
as if my son became a twisted rope
fought over in a frozen tug-of-war,
his dad invisible except for arms
that strain against the silence of the creek.

Ebb Tide

Fluted plastic jugs, their lids aslant,
tissue boxes, beakers of cold beige tea,
flowers on cards on pin boards. Opposite,

one woman warbles Vera Lynn all night
softly through her mask; another,
hair Belle Colour black, tucks her earphones

tight, and in the next bed, Mother,
skewered with a transverse nail,
clings to a photo of her rib-thin cat.

The surgeon consults his tables
like a clairvoyant, divining
the ebb and flow of pain, while I

measure days by the state of the tide
all along the railway to Shoeburyness,
where we hiss to a stop, just short of the sand.

Vigil

Cradling your head like a newborn's, I tilt
the cup against your lips, drip feeding
what emotions? Numbering the lives
that ended since the day I found your door
ajar and searched each room but only met
a smell of gas, an emptiness. I dressed
your shin where skin as ragged as old silk
ripped and poured blood, gaped open like the mouth
I wipe after each sip. There are still words
to say to the clear spaces in your mind
but how to know the moment when you'll leave?
Searching your vacant eyes for a reprieve,
I whisper through the hum of the machines
and will my words into your empty dreams.

Eulogy For A Soldier

His coat hangs in the hall cupboard,
a uniform in one sole garment: epaulettes,
caped shoulders, a checked woollen lining
that reinforced him on cold days, with belts

on waist and sleeves to guarantee
the proper fit, and every button sewn

secure in place. Long years of service
have dulled the fabric to a washed-out grey,

thin as the sky that afternoon, when
they stretchered him in and the surgeon said,

'this one's a waste of time.' Grey as the stones

he laid, forty years on, to make a terrace
where he could sit on Sundays, watching

his children's children with his one good eye,
mindful of his kit. Mindful of time.

Lives We Have Lost

Across the courtyard behind St-Joseph,
I look into the window of my neighbour
five metres on. Each evening, the light
pierces her apartment from the street beyond

and frames her with the lambency
of a small icon, stilled in time,
appearing as she might have done
viewed through a folding, half-plate

camera lens, in 1900, its bellows
compacting on themselves,
as rooms compress the centuries.
And so, I can believe that every one

who ever set his foot here must have left
something of himself, an image
printed on the veil of these old rooms,
like holding cells for spirits. Yet

in England, when I try to track my father
in the house I once called home, each space
echoes absence. I look for him, unable
to believe there's nothing left

in this room where he sat each day
– if I used my camera on the scene,
I'd call this composition *Salt* –
or at the tallboy where he kept the shirts

I bought him, still encased in cellophane
(*Humility* would be appropriate), and wonder
why all those unknown souls in France should seem
more real than he does in this silent place.

Mistral

A shutter's coming loose across the street.
At Carrefour Bar we watch it swing and turn
in silence between blows. Small flakes, green
as olives, spiral from the crash of stone
on slatted wood and fall, forever lost,
like echoes of last summer's fluting notes,
or leavings on your plate, that turn to rust
when shaded through a glass of palest rose.

A woman from the Bar Aux Huiles unpleats
her blind with noiseless fingers, as the birds
call shrill among the plane tree's fading leaves,
yet still we sit, and wait, and have no words;
unsure if one should leave, the other stay,
until the waiter whispers. "*Terminé?*"